MIND YOUR CHILD'S ART

A Guide for Parents and Teachers

MIND
YOUR CHILD'S
ART

A Guide
for Parents and Teachers

BY

Laura Bannon

With 14 illustrations in color
and 52 in black and white

PELLEGRINI & CUDAHY
PUBLISHERS · NEW YORK

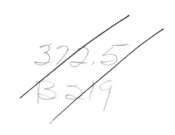

ACKNOWLEDGEMENT

THE AUTHOR AND PUBLISHER of this book wish to express their
appreciation to Field Enterprises, Inc., for their courtesy in
granting permission to reproduce from the plates of the children's drawings and paintings used in this book. This includes
52 illustrations in black and white and 14 illustrations in color.
These originally appeared in an earlier edition of their publica-
tion, CHILDCRAFT—Volume 13 on "Arts and Music."

*

All of the children's pictures were produced in the School of the
Art Institute of Chicago while Laura Bannon was director of
the Junior Department under the deanship of Norman Rice.
The book also includes line drawings by the author.

FOREWORD

THE ART OF CHILDREN is now widely discussed, but it is still widely misunderstood. Of the many words that have been written on this subject, few have attempted to guide parents intelligently between the extremes of worshipping the young genius on one hand, and the embarrassment of the unexpected and inexplicable on the other. Child art is not adult art. But its logic and charm afford a means of insight into the nature of all art, and what is perhaps more important, into the nature of the individual at a moment when his verbal tools are not fully developed, but his ideas are abundant and complete. At such a moment, pictorial expression may become a satisfying channel of comment from the young mind to the mature observer. If the channel is kept open and free, there is an opportunity for communication of a special and rewarding kind. If the channel is closed by raillery or adult blindness the loss is irreparable.

Parents who read this book are fortunate to have as their guide a teacher who understands both the nature of her subject and the human beings she has taught. Out of her extensive and varied experience, as painter, teacher, author and illustrator, Laura Bannon has achieved deep awareness of the values she discusses. She has ably taught both children and their teachers, and has guided a children's art program in the Saturday classes of the School of the Art Institute of Chicago with notable success. A good many of the young people she has had in her charge have continued active work in the visual arts and are now practicing artists, designers, teachers and craftsmen. But a great many more have surely benefited from the serious (though never solemn) judgment she and her associates brought to the consideration of each child's work. To every child she has given guidance without domination. If they have chosen other outlets for their adult energies, at least they respect the arts and share in their enjoyment. They are heirs to the best the world can produce.

In a world which is trying hard to regain its self confidence, we may well consider the importance of helping every individual to evaluate the quality of his own creative thinking. Parents and teachers have a common responsibility in this matter. Surely books like this one will bring into clear focus both the nature of the problem and one of its pleasant by-products, the art of children.

NORMAN RICE

SYRACUSE UNIVERSITY

JULY 14, 1952

MIND YOUR CHILD'S ART

A Guide for Parents and Teachers

LOOK AGAIN at those scribbled drawings before you toss them into the wastebasket. That sheet of squares and curlicues, which kept Johnny quiet for five whole minutes, may be the most inventive thing he has done in all his four years.

Of course, you must be able to read the signs in order to understand the drawings. If you have the notion that all good pictures must be realistic you will be blind to the vital qualities of child art. You will say the wrong things when you want to encourage Johnny. You may hinder when you mean to help.

If you clear your mind of grown-up ideas about pictures and put yourself in Johnny's place, you will share in the fun of his creative efforts and you can be a help in their development. Your most difficult task will be to say nothing at the right time.

When Johnny first begins to scribble with a pencil it is new to him. He finds it entertaining enough just to see the black line trail along behind this strange stick. If you give him a large crayon that leaves a strong black trail he will like that even better.

The paper should be inexpensive because he will use so much of it. The back of leftover wall-paper or a roll of white shelf paper can be

used. Cut it in lengths of from sixteen to twenty-four inches. He will also be happy scribbling on the cardboard that came with the laundry, or the back of that advertisement that arrived in the morning mail. If it folds or curls, thumbtack it to a piece of Beaverboard, Gypsum-board, or a wood board soft enough to take the thumbtacks. Be sure the paper is large, for Johnny hasn't as yet developed the muscular control necessary for small drawings.

Johnny won't try to draw pictures at once. And you won't speed up the process by drawing a stick man for him to copy. He will probably reward any such interference by dropping the whole matter to play with his train. Why not? You have spoiled his fun just when he was finding out all the things that can be done with a pencil or crayon. When he is ready to do so he will draw a man that is very satisfactory,

at least to Johnny. His drawing will be sure to have more character than that stick man you drew. Johnny's attempt will be original.

When he tires of the black crayon, give him a colored one. It is pretty exciting for a child to discover for the first time that he has the power to change a pure white surface to red.

When this experience becomes commonplace to him, Johnny may decide his scribbles stand for something. "This is a boy," he will say. Or, "This is a snowman."

Don't deflate his pride by saying, "Where? I don't see any snowman." Instead, say, "How fine to draw a snowman! You might put a hat on him."

The first time Johnny is given a box of different colored crayons he may, again, spend quite some time just scribbling, showing no interest whatever in drawing pictures. He is getting acquainted with the behavior of colors when they are put together. This kind of play with materials precedes his drawing just as his prattling came before his first words. Even after he has drawn capable pictures with pencil, chalk, or crayon, he will daub and puddle when he first uses wet paint because it behaves differently from the other mediums. A blob of blue paint touches a blob of red and, like magic, there is a spot of purple.

When paint is used the paper should be absorbent enough to keep the color from running excessively. Sheets of white, cream, and gray construction paper, measuring eighteen by twenty-four inches, can be bought at art supply stores. For an inexpensive cream paper ask for

Manila. Bogus paper is an inexpensive gray paper. This is the paper used for most of the child art shown in this book. These pictures are greatly reduced in size, of course.

Prepared poster paint, or tempera paint, comes in jars. This is an opaque water color. It is usually not pure enough in color to make the orange, green, and purple by mixing with red, yellow, and blue. It is best to buy a jar of all six colors. Johnny will also make good use of a jar of white and one of black.

You can, if you like, buy paint in powder form to be mixed with water. In that case keep it quite thick for early painting experiences. Just thin enough to spread easily on the paper.

Transparent water color in pans makes an unhappy choice for this age. The paint is difficult to handle and the effect is not strong enough for a child's big paintings.

If you can afford to do so, buy a large water-color brush (number 9, 10, or larger) for each jar of paint. When every color has its brush it is easier to keep the colors clean. Have a large jar of water on hand to clean a brush that has been dirtied. And have a paint rag to dry it.

Chalk is also a good medium if the colors are strong and the chalks are soft enough to spread easily on the paper. Manila and bogus paper can be used for the chalks as well as for paint.

A child will find the floor quite convenient for his picture making. He likes to work at his picture from different angles. Then, too, if he is using paint it is less apt to run when on a flat surface. A low table makes an ideal working space. Many children enjoy using an easel. That blackboard, which has been so useful for drawing, can be used for an easel. Just tape the paper to it.

When the young artist wears a smock or apron and the working space is covered with newspaper, it isn't necessary to interrupt constantly with "Be careful." Only a reasonable amount of tidiness should be expected. It is, however, time for Johnny to do something else when he becomes less interested in the medium than he is in making a mess.

When Johnny learns to control the paint, he may make orderly arrangements of daubs and lines. This doesn't mean he is going to be

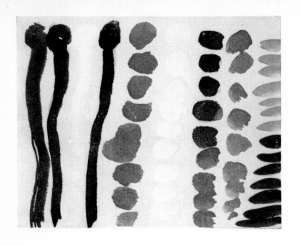

an abstractionist. He is just gaining skill in his play with the medium. The painting at left was done by a four-year-old boy after many hours of puddling.

Johnny's first pictures will probably emerge from a mass of scribbles and daubs. This was true of Mary, age five. When she painted the picture below, she attached lines to the blobs of paint and said, "These are balloons flying through the air."

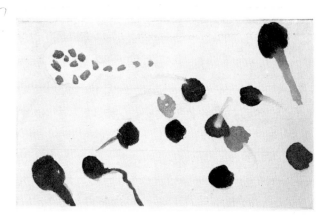

In the painting below, Billy scribbled through the center of his paper with a soft pencil, "Toot, toot!" he cried. "Here comes the train." A minute later the same picture changed to "A big fish in the water." Billy's sound effects likewise changed to those of swishing water.

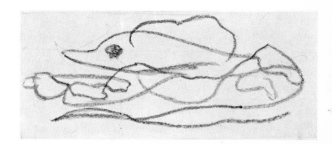

JOAN
age 5

Snow White and
Her Dishes

Your Johnny will soon begin to draw and paint with a definite idea of what he wants to put into his pictures. He will not need, nor want, criticism of these early efforts. He should be allowed to continue working in the spirit of play. All he requires is a comfortable working situation in a happy atmosphere. You might invite his playmates to join him for he will find it stimulating to work with other children of his age.

Don't expect young children to concentrate long on a single picture. Their span of interest is short. They finish painting one idea quickly and are ready to start another. Help them to have confidence in themselves by letting them know that you feel their pictures are worthwhile but don't question them too much about their work.

When Johnny first begins to draw and paint, there are so many things for him to learn and become accustomed to. He not only has to cope with strange mediums. Just the act of putting an idea on paper is new to him.

If Johnny's native abilities are to be developed, he must begin by expressing himself in his own way. He is, from the first, a distinct personality and he should be allowed to remain so. Johnny will put the things from his intimate little world into his pictures. He will draw houses, flowers, trees, sky, sun, birds, animals, and people, in a manner peculiar to all child art. Yet he will have his own individual style in working with these symbols.

Johnny will probably draw large the things that are of greatest interest to him—the things that seem important. The people in his early pictures are apt to have oversize heads. He may put in all the facial features, even when he has left out the body. Has not Johnny watched his parents' faces since he first opened his eyes? Is it not the face that laughs, cries, talks, and is fed? Bodies are of less consequence. Sometimes, in the absence of the body, arms and legs are joined to the head. If hands and feet are shown the small artist will probably develop them only as much as is necessary to give the idea.

You may think that a picture should always imitate the actual appearance of the thing it represents. You are convinced that a house should be larger than a man, even in a six-year-old's drawing, and you assume that your child should work for proportion from the first. You mean to help Johnny when you say, "You have drawn the man's head too large," or, "Where are the man's hands?"

Now, Johnny is quite happy drawing pumpkin heads on his people, and he hasn't the slightest interest in proportion at this stage of his de-

velopment. If he feels you do not approve of his efforts, he will find something else to do.

"Well," you may say, "Art doesn't run in our family. We don't expect Johnny to be an artist anyway."

But you do want him to have many outlets for self-expression, just because they are necessary to mental health and happiness. Drawing, like singing and dancing, is a natural means of expression. Any normal child feels the joy of it and may continue to do so if his efforts are met with understanding.

If you study Johnny's pictures, you will find that he looks at his surroundings with a point of view quite different from yours. For instance, you are accustomed to think of the sky and ground as meeting at the horizon but that is not Johnny's conception of his little world. He will probably show the sky in a strip across the top of the paper while the ground is a band across the bottom. When we realize Johnny's viewpoint, we must admit it is logical. He thinks in terms of close-up things. His experiences do not extend to the horizon. The sky

The picture at left was painted by Sheldon, age five. He said, "I went to play in the park. My house is across the street."

is over his head, the ground is under his feet, and he is in between, a very important person in the center of things.

Sandy painted the picture on the previous page when he was five. Later in the same year, he drew this small picture at right.

Children show a great interest in active things. They like to paint the sun with its long symbolic rays. Sometimes their drawings show lively smoke streaming from the chimneys of houses that are not developed enough to have roofs or windows. This is true of Sandy's picture above, painted when he was five.

Youngsters are often able to express the excitement of moving things amazingly well. Paul, age six, drew the picture of an airplane below and explained, "The plane is going fast." It certainly is.

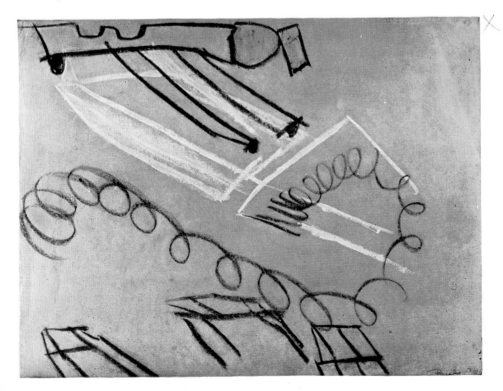

a lion
in the cage,
roaring out
its noise.

Even the houses and their smoke slant with the speed of the passing plane.

Children's drawings sometimes emphasize the essential in a surprising degree. Six-year-old Elizabeth drew the picture above of a lion in a cage. She said, "The lion is roaring out its noise." There in the picture is all the equipment a lion needs for roaring. He has a huge open mouth filled with a tongue and teeth. You will notice, however, that the lion has no hind legs. Now, Elizabeth knows a lion has hind legs and she would probably show them in the picture if she drew a lion running. But, of what importance is the number of legs when a young artist is filled with the excitement of a lion's roar?

Helen, age six, drew the above picture and explained, "The robin is looking for a worm. I saw him yesterday." Does it matter that the houses are only a little larger than the bird? They are merely a backdrop for the central figure, an early spring robin.

When he was seven, John drew the picture below of a pilgrim shooting a turkey. Notice that he has condensed the subject matter of his picture, drawing the all-important turkey extra large.

Most adults expect a picture to show only what it is possible for a person to see at one time. Children are not hampered by this convention. They will show you, in one picture, what is happening inside the house as well as outside it. They sometimes break up objects and show the parts separately. A child often shows, all in one picture, events that happen over a period of time.

Alfred, age five and a half, drew this maplike picture of a weekend trip. He said, "We went north to see my grandfather (see the train along the right-hand side of his picture). The sun was going down (the setting sun is at the top). The men were working

in the field (below the sun). Pumpkins are there (circles above the house). The house was in front of the cornfield. There was a wagon with some twigs near, some hay, and a farmer." The end of the story brings us back to the starting point with a fine economy of space.

Meyer, age six, drew the ghost picture above. The lines around the edge of the picture give the contour of the ghost house, including the front step and doorknob. One of the ghosts floats through the door, another arrives at the foot of the bed. Within the contour of the house, as Meyer explained, "A masked detective drives to the door of the ghost house. He lights a cigarette. A dog coming out of the doghouse barks at him. He laughs."

The story that Johnny tells about his picture should be considered

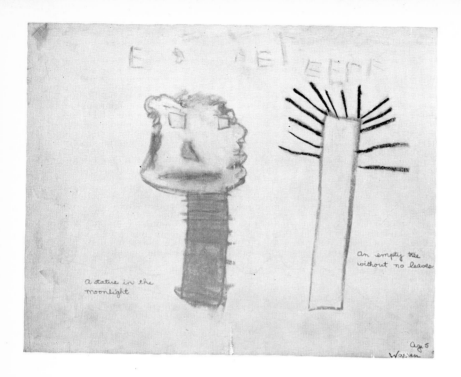

a statue in the
moonlight

an empty tree
without no leaves

Age 5
Warren

together with his drawing as his complete expression. When he is older, he will be more able to draw a picture that explains the whole idea, but in his early efforts the drawing may show you only part of the idea Johnny meant to convey.

The above drawing with its square shapes becomes significant when Warren tells us, "It is a statue in the moonlight and a empty tree without no leaves."

Vance, age four, did some sound thinking when he drew the next picture of an Indian. He tells us that the bird, in the upper right hand corner, gave all its feathers to the Indian for his war bonnet so the bird can't fly and is falling.

Here is the story that Meyer, age five, tells about his picture at the bottom of facing page. Notice how well the literary style, as well as the story content, suits the picture.

26

"A big rock covered with grass. There's a fire on it. The two animals can live a little bit in the fire. The black one can only live in the water—a little on land. It is an olden time animal. Some big ships of mine are coming to explore this land. The black animal is not a whale. It is an olden time animal."

Children have strong emotional reactions to color. It is natural for Johnny to choose bright colors and use primitive color schemes for his early pictures. He is likely to paint with colors that have little or no relation to the actual hues of the objects.

When Johnny first puts yellow and blue paint together and watches it turn green, this is, to him, a potent experience, more convincing than any verbal statement or a stack of color charts. He puts a dab of red beside the green and has an emotional reaction to the color effect. He places this color beside that and some combinations seem more exciting to him than do others. The colors he selects are not the same as those chosen by Bunny or Billy because John was born with his own color sense and it is as individual as that cowlick in his hair. This color sense develops as he works directly with color.

Evan was nine when he painted the picture at the left and explained, "It's a lonely tree with bear tracks going to it."

At the right is nine-year-old Jim's painting, RIDING THE ROLLER-COASTER AT RIVER-VIEW.

28

RIVERVIEW Jim

Richard, age nine, did the chalk drawing above, PEOPLE GOING TO
CHURCH IN THE SNOW. He also did the drawing below, A TRAIN GOING
THROUGH THE MOUNTAINS.

*   *   *

Vacation trips often inspire good pictures. When experiences are
new, interest is high, and so observation is keener. When Meyer, at

the age of six, went on a trip with his family, he and his sister rode in the trailer where they failed to get the best view of everything. So he drew the picture at the left to show the arrangement he would like for the next trip.

In the picture he has drawn an observation tower on top of the trailer. Meyer has a wonderful view from the balcony of the tower where he plays with his toy pistol. With her camera his sister is snapping a picture of a bird in flight. Before her is the pet turtle she took along on the last trip. All this is splendid invention for a child of six.

At this stage of his development, Meyer always drew his people side view with the head and the body in one simple unit. He never drew arms on his people unless they were of immediate use. In the picture above you will see that Meyer drew himself showing only the arm that is used to shoot the gun while his father uses both arms to drive the car. The people in Meyer's pictures were there only for the action they represented, and there was always plenty of action, humor, and little boy thrillers.

In Meyer's seventh year, he began to give his people more character. He then drew the faces front view but he continued to show the side view of the feet. If they were not pressed into action arms were still missing. Notice that, in the picture at the right all idle members of the J. M. BAR RANGE have no arms.

Unlike Meyer, most children draw the front view of a face before attempting the side view. How better to show that a man has two eyes? The feet, however, are usually drawn side view in the early drawings because the shape is more easily explained in that position—a neat trick to avoid foreshortening.

When Johnny is older he will enjoy drawing directly from objects, but during his first three or four years of picture making, he is more likely to call upon his imagination for the subject matter of his pictures. Nevertheless, the things he draws are usually related closely to his direct or indirect experiences.

Do not be baffled by this picture of a lady standing stiffly in the center of a tree top. Sandy, age five, drew it after a woman in his neighborhood walked in her sleep.

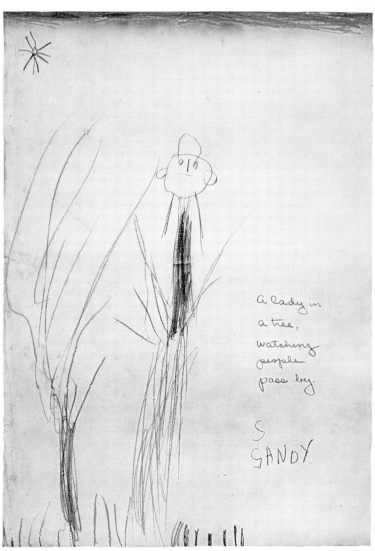

a lady in a tree, watching people pass by.

S
SANDY

To the right is A BRIDGE IN LIN-
COLN PARK *by Joe, age six.*

The Bridge in Lincoln Park

An artist of any age will have more to say about the things of special interest to him and he will express himself more forcefully if he is stirred up emotionally about his subject. So Johnny's best pictures are apt to show the things close to his heart—that new bike, the noisy train that whizzes through the town, or the puppy he loves.

At the bottom of the opposite page is a picture by a seven-year-old boy, painted after he saw a disastrous fire.

At the left is nine-year-old Betty's picture of a pueblo.

James, age seven, showed an unusual interest in drawing land-
scapes viewed from above. The reason for this is explained when, in

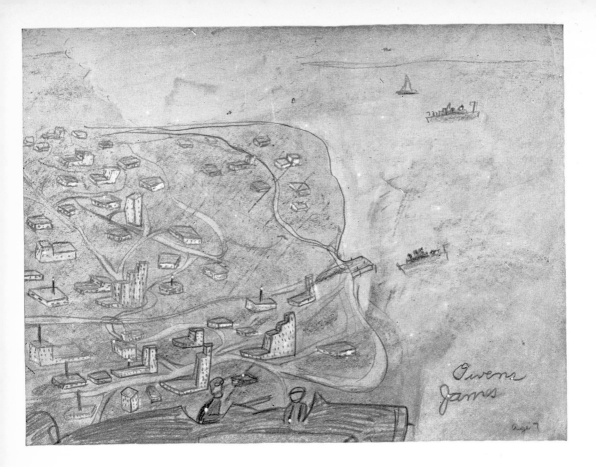

the above picture, James shows himself with his aviator father on one of their many flights.

If Johnny helps shovel the walk after a blizzard, he will put real excitement and perhaps a great deal of factual material into his snow picture. Burton, age 11, drew the picture at the top of the next page after he had helped shovel the family car out of a snowdrift.

If he is a city child and has had no first hand acquaintance with a cow, he may draw it with some logic but with little knowledge of fact. When an artist draws a picture that is not meant to be funny, *don't ever laugh at his efforts.*

If Johnny has a generous amount of humor in his make-up he will draw pictures that are meant to be funny. Of course, you will not expect his humor to be subtle. It is in its early stages of development and will probably be of the slapstick variety.

Encourage Johnny to watch for, and put into his pictures, the amusing happenings of his everyday life. It is a splendid way for him to develop his sense of humor. These funny pictures should be drawn in the same sincere style in which he draws his other pictures.

Children are tempted to copy comic strip characters. These are easy to copy because the drawing is often simple and obvious in its action and the humor is usually at a child's level of understanding. But since children are reasonable beings, it is not too difficult to get them to realize that this kind of imitation will not help them become good cartoonists. A successful cartoonist has his own particular sense of

TROUBLE WITH A
STOVEPIPE *by
William, age 12*

humor and he has invented characters and developed a way of drawing that fits his way of looking upon the amusing side of life. One of
the reasons for his success is that his work is different from that of
other cartoonists.

PITY THE POOR
TEACHER ON
APRIL FOOL'S DAY
by Henry, age 11

If Johnny wants to try his hand at cartooning he should create his own funny characters and work out original comic strips. Below are cartoon characters from Hector's sketch book. He was ten when he drew them.

Johnny may at some time cause you concern because he insists upon drawing the same picture again and again. If he repeatedly draws

a dog but each time he adds new subject matter or paints the picture with different colors, there is no reason to worry. But if his pictures show no development at all, there may be a good explanation for his behavior.

Perhaps Johnny longed to have a picture exhibited at school and, at last, it happened. His picture of a dog was pinned on the wall. The attention Johnny received because of this drawing was pleasant. He wanted more of it so he drew more dog pictures like the first one.

Or maybe you entered Johnny in an art class and there, in front of him and his new classmates, you told the teacher that your Johnny was talented. That put him on the spot and he became afraid he would do a poor picture. He was sure he could draw dogs well, so he drew more of them.

It could be that you showed Johnny's picture to callers while Johnny listened to, and believed, the polite praise of his dog picture. Mrs. Brown may have observed that you were going to have a real artist in the family.

However it happened, it is quite likely that the quality of Johnny's output has somehow become overimportant to him. A standard has been set which he fears he can't live up to unless he uses the old familiar subject matter for his pictures.

If Johnny should get into a rut with his art work, try to interest him in fresh ideas either by conversation about things he likes or by giving him new experiences such as a trip to the lake to see the boats or a jaunt to the railroad yards or to the zoo.

It is well to remember that when Johnny draws and paints creatively the experience he has in doing it is far more valuable than the picture he produces. This work gives him an opportunity for inventive thinking and a chance to develop his sense of space and color.

It is an excellent outlet for self-expression. All this is of primary importance. The finished picture is secondary.

However, Johnny must continue to feel that you are interested in his results. Many of his most sincere efforts should be saved and occasionally a picture of which he is especially proud might be matted and hung in his playroom or bedroom.

There is a happy medium in the amount of favorable comment Johnny should receive. Ask yourself how much praise he needs to keep him drawing to the best advantage.

*   *   *

It is always dangerous to make generalizations about children because they are as individual as grown ups. At about the age of nine or ten years most boys and girls become increasingly critical of their work. They now want to explain ideas more accurately and with greater realism and so they feel the need of greater skill.

Johnny, who has up to now painted all surfaces flat, may struggle to make that silo on his barn "look round," while Sammy may be concerned with putting all the details into a drawing of his bike.

Johnny may need smaller brushes to paint detail. He will want to make pictures of a size and shape to fit the subject matter as well as the use to be made of the pictures. He will find it stimulating to try out different mediums: India ink with a pen or brush, transparent water color or even oil paint.

Oil paint, canvas or canvas board, and the necessary brushes are relatively expensive. And for a youngster they have no great advan-

tage over opaque water color. However, Johnny will paint his best pictures when his interest is high. If he hankers for it to the extent that oil paint will result in a burst of enthusiasm for picture making, and if you can afford it, let him work in oil.

Ronald drew the picture above when he was ten years old. He made many intricate plans for boats, houses, and cities. Pictorial representation didn't especially interest him. He said he wanted to be an architect. Notice the fine sense of pattern and the orderly manner in which he has handled the detail.

Robert painted this picture of the fire engine when he was thirteen. Here we have an attempt to draw objects in perspective from three-quarter view as well as an attempt to show rounded forms with shadows. At this point Robert was not interested in learning formal rules of perspective. He wanted only to solve his immediate problems.

Walter approached his picture-making with less emotion than Robert but with more logic. At the age of ten he drew the still life of lab-

oratory equipment below. When he was eleven he was eager to learn the rules of perspective and he wanted a general knowledge of ways to use light and shade to give the appearance of solid form, and so he was given professional instruction in these matters. During this period he painted the church shown in color on page 53.

41

With the help of
his pocket mirror
Harry, age
eleven, painted
this self-portrait
in oil.

Lillian, age twelve,
made the chalk
drawing of herself
and her cat.

42

However, most children aren't ready for such formal information at the age of eleven. It is a mistake to impose this kind of training upon Johnny before he feels the need for it. He will retain only the information that he is able to make a part of his little core of conviction.

Johnny's early work was probably done with a simple, wholehearted directness that gave spontaneity and unity to his pictures. As he grows older and becomes more self-conscious, more analytical of his work, it may lose some of its former charm. Just as parts of his body may grow at different rates and seem out of proportion and uncoordinated for a time, so his pictures may fall apart in design because they develop unevenly in their different phases.

Occasionally an adolescent child approaches his art work with such force of feeling that it doesn't lose any of its former esthetic qualities. But if an awkward stage occurs, any attempt to avoid it is an attempt to keep a youngster from the growth necessary for a more mature expression. If he continues to be interested in drawing and painting, unity will probably return to his work when he has conquered the complicated problems of representation.

Johnny will no longer be satisfied with the primitive color schemes that served him very well during his first years of painting. In his early pictures he depended largely upon his feeling for color. Now he uses his reason to a greater extent. He will want to mix the exact shade of green to paint that new bike and he will struggle to get the

Mary was eleven years old when she painted this picture with opaque water-color. She calls it A PARADE.

right color in the background of the picture so the bike will "show off" well.

As Johnny struggles with these problems he gains a conscious control over color and he develops his color perceptions. A well-rounded color sense is his right and it can become one of his most precious possessions. His growing awareness of nature's wise use of color will be a source of joy all his life.

We hope Johnny will not grow up with the color prejudices that

Eliza, age nine, calls her picture MY PUPPIES.

assail many adults. Through working with it, he will learn that no color is bad in itself. It can be good or bad only in its relation to other colors or in the use made of it. When he furnishes a home or selects a wardrobe his choice of color will reflect his own character.

Irwin at the age of ten painted this picture of the water buffaloes. Notice the close relation of color, space, and line arrangement. No small space or line can be found that is not in keeping with the mood of the picture. This cannot be accidental and yet it was done with no conscious thought of design. Irwin had sketched actual mounted water buffaloes at a museum. Later he drew them again from memory, fitting them into an imaginary setting.

Any art training that underestimates this inborn sense of design and does not aim to nurture it carefully, can only be a hindrance to cultural development.

The parent, the librarian, the grade school teacher, the scout director—anyone who directs free activity that includes drawing and painting—can ask the questions and make the suggestions that keep a child's ideas spilling out on paper. But, unless qualified professionally to do so, it is better not to attempt criticisms on proportion, perspective, composition, and design. And please keep hands off a child's work.

Know that within Johnny there is much that hungers for development through expression. If he is held back by lack of faith in himself, your sympathy and praise will help dissolve his fears. Have faith in his ability to create. Urge him to do things his own way, not to worry about the way others draw and paint.

Help Johnny to a keen awareness of the subjects and ideas for pictures that are almost anywhere he looks. A picture may begin with a trip to the grocery, a stop to watch a street excavation, a man up a pole working on telephone wires, a dish of ice-cream at the corner drugstore, a wind storm, or meeting Aunt Minnie at the railroad station.

Events more remote, but remembered vividly because of emotional stress, often produce pictures straight from the heart. Here are some titles that will start Johnny and his friends chattering about the things they remember:

Jackie, age eleven,
painted
A RIVER SCENE
remembered
from his summer's
vacation.

THE DAY I GOT LOST

MY KITTEN COULDN'T CLIMB DOWN FROM THE TREE

OUR HOUSE CAUGHT ON FIRE

OUR BALL TEAM WON AN IMPORTANT GAME

GRANDMOTHER FELL DOWN STAIRS

George, age ten, drew
A TRIP BY AUTOMOBILE.

WE WERE SNOWED IN AT OUR CABIN

A FIRE DRILL AT SCHOOL

MY FIRST TWO-WHEELER

I SAW THE CIRCUS

A BOAT TRIP UP THE RIVER

I MADE A SPEECH AT CHURCH

A TURKEY CHASED ME

I FED THE HORSES AT UNCLE JIM'S FARM

WE BUILT A SNOW FORT

OUR PUPPET SHOW

WE ALL TOOK OUR DOLLS TO SCHOOL

MY FIRST HAIRCUT IN A BARBER SHOP

WE MOVED TO A NEW HOUSE

I SAW A BUILDING TORN DOWN

MOTHER AT SEWING MACHINE

HELPING WASH THE DISHES

A BUNCH OF FLOWERS

A GAME OF TAG

Allow the boys and girls to talk about their experiences until their interest is high, then get them to draw by saying, "Tell us about it by making pictures."

TWO LADIES *by*
Marion age 11

The older children who have sufficient concentration enjoy making pictures that use the same subject matter in different situations:

THE WAY I LOOK IN MY OLD HAT

THE WAY I LOOK IN MY NEW HAT

WHEN I HAD LONG HAIR

AFTER MY HAIR WAS CUT

BEFORE WE DECORATED FOR CHRISTMAS

AFTER WE DECORATED FOR CHRISTMAS

Norman, age 11 got his subject matter for this painting from a movie he had seen.

OUR HOUSE BEFORE THE SNOW STORM

OUR HOUSE AFTER THE SNOW STORM

VIEW FROM MY WINDOW IN SPRING

VIEW FROM MY WINDOW IN FALL

DURING THE RAIN

HOW I LOOKED WITH THE MUMPS

HOW I LOOKED WITH THE MEASLES

Here are titles that encourage a child to search within himself, examining his own feelings:

I'M SCOWLING BECAUSE I'M ANGRY

I'M SCOWLING BECAUSE I'M THINKING HARD

I'M SCARED AND SCREAMING

I'M SCARED AND WHISTLING

I'M SCARED AND LISTENING

LAUGHING BECAUSE I'M HAPPY

LAUGHING JUST TO TEASE

TIRED BUT STILL WORKING

THROUGH WORKING, RELAXED AND SLEEPY

Try, FILLED WITH AN ACHE, or a picture that shows no rainbow but is called, LOOK! A RAINBOW IN THE SKY! The young cartoonist will like, FUNNY FACES I CAN MAKE. Johnny and his friends will think of many more titles along this line.

Here is a suggestion for pictures that begin with a different way of "feeling." Place objects in a box or behind a curtain—objects such as a toy animal, an ink bottle, a wrapped package, a flower, a bell and a book. Lead the artist blindfolded to the objects. Let him feel them, then draw the mental pictures that come to him. Youngsters like this game after they realize that it is not a test to see how close they can come to picturing the real object but, instead, to use the shapes of the unseen objects just to start pictures forming in their imaginations.

A game that is much the same can be played with fanciful, and sometimes amusing, results. Scents have a way of stirring the memory and the imagination. Let one child smell an unseen flower, another an apple, another an onion, etc. Each makes a picture stimulated by the scent.

Although much progress has been made, cultural education, in many of our schools, is unfortunately still hampered by methods that are based on false assumptions. These methods assume that Johnny has nothing esthetic to be developed. He is, supposedly, just a receptacle for information that is parceled out to him for the purpose of aiding him in producing a certain picture. (The nature of the picture has been planned in advance by the art teacher or art supervisor.)

Johnny is guided step by step to draw, we shall say, a rabbit. He must leave behind him his individual observations of and feelings about rabbits even though his own

approach might have more vigor than the adult conception he is asked to copy. Oh, he may be given the opportunity to decide whether or not he will show the rabbit eating a carrot or he might be allowed to tinker with the background. But, if he is an obedient little boy, the chances are that his picture will look enough like that of his forty classmates to fit nicely into a continuous border around the room.

This has been worse than a negative experience for Johnny. It has been damaging, as anyone can testify who tries to get him to do creative work after a few years of the above training.

Another type of art lesson often taught in our schools allows Johnny more freedom but sometimes has the disadvantage of expecting him to make pictures of things that are foreign to him. This situation is apt to occur when the art lessons are correlated or integrated with other lessons such as geography or history.

Now it is quite possible that, through his school work, motion pictures, and television Johnny has had enough indirect experience with subjects, such as American Indians, Pilgrims, and cowboys, to draw

Feeling the full responsibility for the outcome of his picture Robert, age 12, relived the thrill of seeing a train go by when he drew the picture on page 52. Walter painted the church above when he was ten. Emily was also ten when she drew the picture below showing herself reading about Lincoln.

creatively. Too often, however, he is required to spend his art period drawing the costumes and dwellings of a land he has never seen, and so it is necessary for him to resort to other pictures for his information. This procedure may teach geography to Johnny but it should not take the place of his creative art work.

If Johnny's school fails to provide him with good instruction in art, you may consider placing him in the class of adults taught by Mr. Blake, the portrait painter. This solution may also be unwise. Johnny should not skip so lightly over the natural interests and outlook of a youngster, to be plunged into an objective study of models and still life. Then, too, there is the possibility that Mr. Blake's sole viewpoint on teaching is to get students to paint pictures just as he does.

Johnny's teacher should have a broad enough knowledge of the field of art to realize that there are many directions in which the boy's talents might move. It is also necessary that his teacher understand the manner in which child art develops.

Perhaps you find that in your community it is not possible for Johnny to get the right kind of professional art training under an instructor and so you look for aid in the book stores. You will find books and sets of charts containing explicit directions on how to go about drawing a cat, a figure, a horse, etc. But most of these ready-made solutions will eventually prove to be a hindrance rather than a help to Johnny's art education.

For example, a chart that shows how to draw a horse may help Johnny produce a horse picture that will win praise from the casual observer, but the chart acted only as a crutch. Johnny's picture of the horse is not entirely the result of his own skill. The artist who prepared the chart did most of the work for him. Copying the picture from the flat surface of the chart is much easier than drawing it on the flat paper after looking at the round forms of a real horse.

A good instructor would help Johnny to understand the structure behind the forms and so make it easier for him to draw the horse in his own manner from any position. If Johnny wants to learn more about drawing horses and has no chance for professional instruction, he should learn by drawing from real horses.

Hector makes use of a convenient model when he draws this picture of a horse and calls it "Lunch time for a milk horse."

Here are more drawings from ten-year-old Hector's sketch book. They are good examples of sincerity. To look at his sketch book is to become acquainted with Hector. The boy's family and home surroundings, his friends, his neighborhood, and his school, are all shown in a style that could be only Hector's.

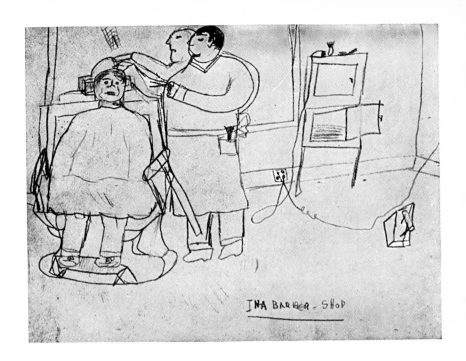

Johnny's progress in his drawing and painting need not stop because he fails to receive the best instruction. If he enjoys drawing the things around him, he has found one of the best sources for study.

If Johnny continues to improve in the different phases of his picture making and if he maintains a sincere way of working, that is in harmony with his character, you may be sure that he is developing in the right direction.

Robert, age eleven, painted the bottom picture of himself asleep in his room.

John, age ten, lives in a large city. He painted the picture of an elevated train on the following page.

Kenneth, age 7, painted THE RESCUE after hearing reports of flood conditions over the radio.

Robert, age 7, drew A LADY I KNOW.

Everett, age 12, drew his idea of an Irishman at lower left of preceding page.

Audrey, age 12, sketched people who posed for her, on page 60.

Jack, age 11, painted SNOW-BOUND after a storm had left his home half buried in snow.

May was eleven when she drew the rhythmic picture of her cats.

Remember that we are not necessarily trying to make an artist of Johnny. If he should choose to be one, we have helped him on his way by allowing him to develop those qualities within himself that are essential to his individual expression. But qualities such as a developed sense of color and space, a habit of keen visual observation, and self-confidence, are basic in many walks of life.

Child art, when encouraged to expand creatively, aids in building character and a capacity for a broader, happier life.